(My eldest son told me to write "I'm a legend!")

This book has been written by a highly qualified and very experienced manager, who worked in various private customer service and public service roles, over several decades.

Some of the staff managed by the author could be described as judgmental, wilful, authoritarian, stubborn, confident, assertive, entitled, para-legal, para-military or litigious. (We can only imagine how they would describe the author!)

The author completed all of the high-level leadership courses offered by their well-established, public organisation. One course was an interstate senior management leadership development course, with international attendees. Another course matched the author with a rotary and business mentor. The author also mentored numerous people within the author's workplaces.

The author seeks to assist other managers, by providing "pearls of wisdom", and sharing observations and lessons learnt from experience (generally the hard way!).

The author wishes:

- to save managers from embarrassment and frustration;
- to assist managers to be more productive and avoid pitfalls;
- they had been able to read this book, before embarking on their management career (as that might have led to skyrocketing promotions!); and
- that all who read this book have fruitful management careers.

I would like to dedicate this book:

- (and apologise to) my family, including my three beautiful children, for the time that I dedicated to my work and study; and
- to those who assisted with proofreading the various drafts (e.g. Hiamy).

Dave A. P. Smith

RELATABLE MANAGEMENT TIPS

AUSTIN MACAULEY PUBLISHERS™

LONDON • CAMBRIDGE • NEW YORK • SHARJAH

A CIP catalogue record for this title is available from the British Library.

ISBN 9781035800865 (Paperback)
ISBN 9781035800872 (ePub e-book)

www.austinmacauley.com

First Published 2024
Austin Macauley Publishers Ltd®
1 Canada Square
Canary Wharf
London
E14 5AA

I would like to acknowledge my staff and managers for the learning challenges and experiences, that provided me with ample fodder for this book (and for putting up with me, as I learnt the hard way).

Table of Contents

Introduction

Organisations and businesses may vary, but there are overarching business management principles, which can be applied to them.

Most businesses have:

- staff;
- customers;
- key stakeholders;
- to deliver a product or service;
- to meet targets/objectives;
- a budget; and
- to maximise profits/productivity.

Therefore, all managers need certain skills, including being financially savvy and able to set direction, monitor achievement and manage staff.

This book:

- seeks to equip managers, by providing them with common sense business management principles, to guide their decision-making and actions;

- is written in a simplistic, easy-to-read format;
- provides practical tips for busy new managers;
- includes relatable examples, to help demonstrate the principles; and
- could be used by mentors, to generate conversation and develop up-and-coming managers.

Applying these principles may help managers to avoid:

- injuring their staff;
- damaging their own, or the organisation's, reputation;
- wasting time; and
- creating unnecessary distractions from desired outputs.

Know Where You Sit

"Have you ever seen a Galileo thermometer working? That is what staff movement in an organisation can look like". You need to ascertain and maintain current awareness of where you sit within your business structure. Know who your team, manager, customers and key internal stakeholders are. You need to build productive working relationships with them. Ascertain what they would like from you, what they want to achieve and what they are working on. This will help you determine your approach, priorities and who you could collaborate with. Stakeholder liaison could raise issues that require your attention. In any event, these relationships will provide you with information sources. They may even identify opportunities for your career advancement (e.g. secondments, mentors, upgrading, promotions, etc.). This advice, under "Know where you sit", could also form part of an interview answer to the question "What would you do in your first 90 days in a new role?"

Follow the Process

Be aware of, and comply with, your corporate policies and procedures. They have usually been developed over time, from lessons learnt, and reflect contemporary best practice. The policies will have been endorsed by management, so they provide protection for your actions. Following policy removes some of the emotion when dealing with issues and could protect you from allegations that you were biased. Furthermore, the need to follow established procedures is enshrined in administrative law (Procedural fairness).

Get Your Powder Dry

It is easy to fall into the trap of believing the first person who tells you something. However, before you prejudge and take action, you should make additional inquiries. Keep an open mind. Ascertain the facts (Get your powder dry). There are generally two sides to a story. Administrative law also requires that, where you are about to make a decision that is not favourable to a person, you give them an opportunity to be heard on the matter.

Consult the SME

Organisations generally have employees, Subject Matter Experts (SME), who specialise in a field and give advice in the area that they specialise in. Their speciality may be Equity and Diversity, Ethical Conduct, Human or Industrial Relations, etc. When dealing with an issue, consult these SME. The SME services are generally already being paid for by the organisation, so you should use this available resource. Consulting with SME will provide you with authority and support for your decisions. Otherwise, the person that you are impacting may complain to the SME. In that case, the SME may subsequently overturn your decision and undermine your credibility.

For example, managers should make an SME-agreed plan to deal with staff who, for whatever reason, are unable to perform the duties of their role. The plan may involve giving the staff member additional training, supervision or mentoring, or time for medical treatment and a medical clearance. The plan should allow for the collection of evidence to demonstrate that the staff member was given a fair and reasonable opportunity to meet the required work standard. Otherwise, substantial time may pass, with others carrying the staff member's workload. This may jeopardise the wellbeing of other staff. No one should expect to be paid for work that they are not completing on an indefinite basis.

Don't Take the Monkey

I learnt the "Don't take the monkey" concept whilst undertaking the "Leader as Coach" program. When a staff member comes to you with an issue, they are likely to want to pass you the issue and have you resolve it. Do not take the monkey off their back and put it on to yours (unless absolutely necessary). Work should not flow up! Instead, mentor and coach your staff. Ask them questions that assist them to work out a plan to deal with the issue. One way to achieve this is to lead them through the GROW model (Goal, Reality, Options and Way forward). This will professionally develop and upskill your staff. Your staff will then be better equipped to assist and develop their own staff. Make sure that you have follow-up appointments with the staff member until the issue is resolved. That way, you can confirm that the issue is not festering, and the staff member will not feel like you have left them to their own devices.

Don't Burn Your Bridges

You don't know whom others know (six degrees of separation). Be smart about what you tell others. One day, one of your employees may be your boss or your child's boss. People can open doors for you, or they can close doors on you. You may need that person to be your referee in the future. Even if you move, your reputation can follow you.

If you are leaving a work area, perhaps the grass will not be greener at your new work location. You may want to return to your old work location, i.e., don't burn the virtual relationship bridge when you leave, as you may need that bridge to cross back again.

You should treat people with respect and dignity, even if you are performance managing them. You should be happy to see someone that you work with, in a social setting, by chance (Even when you are with someone that you would like to impress). We all need other people. It would be impossible to maintain society's current living standard if we had to make and do everything ourselves.

If you really don't like someone, "Fake it till you make it". Treat them like they are a good friend and watch how well they respond. There is usually at least one thing good in everybody that you can focus on.

"I learnt not to burn my bridges way too late. I think I went around with my own personal flamethrower, scorching every bridge and person that I came into contact with (until I could not move in any direction). I finally realised that, even if I was the president, prime minister or a monarch, I would still need the co-operation of others".

Respect the Umpire

When decisions do not go your way, you must control your frustration and disappointment. For example, if you unsuccessfully apply for a job. There are always many more disappointed job applicants than happy selectees. You do not know all of the factors at play. You may not be the biggest fish in the applicant net, at that time. Responding poorly will not only not get you that job but it may also prevent you from getting the next one.

"Have you ever watched a child's basketball game, where a child received a foul and then verbally abused the umpire? Did that reverse the decision, or did it just spiral into the player getting fouled off the court entirely?"

Play the Ball, Not the Player

There is a saying in sport that you should play the ball and not the player. This can apply in business too. If you have to give someone adverse feedback, you should not attack or insult them personally. You should focus on criticising the person's behaviour. If you focus on the person's behaviour, it should not matter who the player is, their colour, gender, race or sexual orientation. Therefore, playing the ball can protect you from being accused of discrimination or favouritism.

You Are Unlikely to Be in the Huddle

In sport, a huddle is the team gathering around for a chat. At work, when you were a team member, you may have liked standing around with workmates, "chewing the fat" and getting the latest gossip. However, once you are promoted to management, this is likely to change. If you start going in for the huddle, you may be treated like an outsider and asked what you are doing there. Often, it is management that the team want to talk about. When you are a manager, you are not on the same level as a team member, and your relationships will necessarily change.

Swim Like a Duck

There will be times when you will be extremely busy. Someone may walk into your office, when you are really pressed for time. You may want to snap at them. Alternatively, you may be being badgered by the media, etc. No matter what the situation is do not lose your composure. Losing your composure will not assist. "Instead, swim like a duck. Ducks appear to float calmly and effortlessly along the river while, underneath the water, they are paddling rapidly".

Ask Questions

Don't be afraid to ask questions, particularly when you are new to a role. A common trait of great leaders is humility. You can either pretend to know everything, or be humble enough to ask questions and actually learn. It is better to know how you could find out if you did need to know something. (For example, know who to ask or how to research.)

"I placed a lot of unnecessary stress on myself when I thought that managers had to appear to know everything. It left me feeling awkward about what I could say. Once I realised that no one knows, or can know, everything, I was a lot more relaxed and could behave authentically".

Asking questions can challenge the status quo. Just because something has always been done like that, doesn't mean that it should always continue to be done like that. As examples, thankfully, "someone must have questioned whether Thalidomide, Agent Orange and asbestos should continue to be used". (Thalidomide was found to cause serious birth defects, Agent Orange was found to cause various diseases and asbestos was found to cause mesothelioma cancer.)

Asking questions avoids you making accusations based on your assumptions. For example, "You didn't make an entry about that!" versus "Did you make an entry about that?" Questions may also reveal gaps when people are trying to hide something, trick or bluff you. For example, Can you please show me/walk me through the process?

Put Yourself in Others' Shoes

This principle is about empathy. Whenever you are considering making a change, try stepping into the impacted person's shoes. Think about how they may be affected, what they might think and what they might need to know. Thinking through the change from the impacted person's point of view will assist to ensure that the change is achievable and determine the rationale that should be communicated with the change.

The News Test

When an issue is raised, think about how it could be sensationalised or spun. Could it become the leading news story? What might be the headline on the front page of the newspaper? For example, "Detective Torches Police Car"? Thinking about how an issue may be sensationalised will help determine the level of risk, the proportionate response and the urgency to attend to the matter. You should also make sure that you do not overreact (use a sledgehammer to crack a walnut). An overreaction may be to write an instruction and send it out in an organisation-wide email, to address something that is likely to be a one-off occurrence.

People May Forget
What You Said

There is a saying that people may not remember what you said, but they will remember how you made them feel. "If you had a big argument with someone a long time ago, do you remember the exact details of what you fought about?" You probably don't. You are more likely to remember how you felt, and possibly still feel, towards that person. Consequently, you should always endeavour to make people feel valued and special.

Don't Just Do It (Tell People About It Too!)

I used to just do my work well and expect that others would notice. I thought that the reward and recognition would come. Now, I know that is just not the case. You also need to tell people about the work that you are doing. This is not about gloating, but it does relate to your reputation and branding. You could become known as a subject matter expert in that field.

When other people know what you are working on, they can link you up with different people, to assist you. Telling others what you are working on avoids other people doing the same work, duplicating and wasting effort. It also prevents other people from taking credit for work that you actually did.

There can be a significant difference between perception and reality. "For example, even in locations where the crime rate is extremely low, people can still feel unsafe. Therefore, just reducing crime is not the answer. Consequently, even in low crime areas, Victoria Police deployed Protective Services Officers to Victorian train stations to provide a visible presence and improve public perceptions of safety targets".

The Torch Test

Before you make a decision or take action, think about whether your decision or action would withstand scrutiny if someone shone a torch on to it. Would it survive external review by an oversight body? If your decision or action would not pass the torch test, do not do it.

Compare Apples with Apples

In business, you will be presented with statistics, graphs, tables, charts, etc. You must be able to interpret and understand the statistics. You need to be sure that you are comparing similar things (comparing apples with apples, not oranges). You should understand the groupings that form the basis of the statistics presented. "For example, some figures could be year to date, while others could be a rolling twelve-month average. Alternatively, figures could be calculated on the number of employees, so the figures may be skewed if you have part time or vacant positions".

Swings and Roundabouts

Your staff may request something from you. If you support them and grant their request (the swing), they may be grateful, loyal, work harder and give you more back (the roundabout). What you miss out on, on the swing, you may pick up on the roundabout. However, if you do not grant the request, your staff may withdraw their discretionary effort and you may lose more in the long term. Obviously, it can't be all swings your staff's way, though.

You Can't Do It All Yourself

There is a saying that leadership is getting things done through people. Some people find it difficult to delegate, but managers need to. You cannot do everything yourself. It is not efficient or effective to try. One of my managers said he would be happy if he had nothing to do but consider the strategic direction and undertake blue sky thinking (which is to generate completely new ideas).

Allowing others to complete work gives them work satisfaction. As per Maslow's hierarchy of needs, people have a need to achieve their full potential (Self-actualisation). Allowing others to complete work also assists with business continuity. It builds the capability of staff to perform your role when you are away. What would happen to your work if you were hit by a bus?

Similar to children, your staff will not learn as much if you do everything for them. Even if your staff only do 50% of what you want done and you have to do the rest, isn't that better than you having to do 100% yourself? When you delegate work, you could set a reminder with sufficient time for you to be able to complete the task, from scratch if you had to. Furthermore, when you set the date for returning the task back to you, make sure that you leave sufficient time for you to check the work, before you have to pass it on, so that you can also meet the deadline.

"One of my subordinates was adamant that his staff could not take on any more work. It was as though he was trying to protect his staff from the evil hierarchy. However, his staff actually wanted projects to work on. They wanted to build their experience and gain examples to assist their own career progression".

Trust, but Validate

I originally assumed that everyone had the same work ethic and follow through that I did. I would send emails and assume that the tasks would be completed just because I had asked. Unfortunately, I learnt that this was just not the case. I had to monitor and follow up tasks. I had to satisfy myself that tasks had been completed. Yes, you should trust your staff, but you should also validate what they tell you.

Book in the Look

You need to establish procedures and processes to monitor work and inspect workplaces. For example, block out days in your calendar for external office visits and inspections (i.e. Book in the look). You may, or may not, advise staff in advance that you are attending at their work location. Sometimes, I worked in their common area for the day, so I was privy to conversations and could observe the workplace culture.

Some ways that you can monitor completion of work include the following:

- face-to-face review meetings;
- requesting written briefings/updates;
- regular management meetings;
- straw sample work inspections;
- monthly reporting;
- quarterly performance statistics reviews; and
- requesting drafts of reports.

Structure Your Structures

Think about your organisation's structures, workflow and effectiveness. Look at your business like it is a complex circuit board. For example, you could make sure there is an equitable ratio of supervisors to staff, or that related work units report to the same supervisor, etc.

"When I commenced in a new role, there was a committee which was attended by keen volunteers but was not achieving the traction that I wanted (One volunteer would sit there knitting). I was conscious not to disrespect the contribution of the community volunteers. So, rather than disband that committee, I created a high functioning steering committee, to sit over the top of that committee and handpicked the key stakeholder attendees.

"Another example of smart structuring is a businessman that I know, who established an Australian Chamber of Commerce. Once his Australian Chamber of Commerce was running successfully, he set up the state Chambers of Commerce underneath and had them report to his Australian Chamber of Commerce".

Keep Staff Work Focused

"One strategic manager that I had introduced a strenuous, onerous, monthly reporting regime. At first, I was shocked. It seemed like staff barely had time to do the work because of the time that it took to report on the work done".

However, what I also noticed was that this kept the staff extremely busy. They were so focused on the work that they had little time to turn on each other, to bully others or to gossip. Another benefit was that the staff were more likely to try and action outstanding pieces of work, rather than have to include them in the monthly report. Furthermore, the new monthly reporting regime rapidly improved the output measurements for my strategic manager.

Tackle Tight Timeframes

Managers often receive urgent work requests which place additional pressure on the workplace. Consequently, managers need strategies to manage delivery within tight timeframes.

Some ways to tackle tight timeframes include checking the timeframe, calling people and getting some heads together.

a) Check the Timeframe

If you are requested to do something urgently, or if a deadline has been overlooked and is imminent, contact the requester. You do not want to place your staff under undue stress to meet tight timelines, unless you have to. There may be some flexibility, wriggle room in the due date. The requester may not realise the amount of work involved or they may have even mistyped the due date.

b) Call the People

When something needs to be done urgently don't just send an email and expect that the receiver will read the email and action it in time. Call ahead to find someone who is available to action the request quickly. It is best to talk directly to the person who will be actioning the task. You can explain the task and avoid them going off on a tangent. You do not want something returned last minute, that is nothing like what you actually need.

c) Get Some Heads Together

When an important report needs to be written urgently do not leave it to one person to come up with the direction, content or recommendations on their own. Support the writer. Get as many key stakeholders around the table as you can with short notice. Brainstorm ideas and record the decisions. That way, the report will just need to be written up. Furthermore, your joint, collaborative report should go through as supported, or with less resistance, due to the stakeholder consultation and collaboration.

Don't Pass the Buck

Staff expectations need to be managed. When staff submit an application that you know is unable to be approved, don't just recommend it and pass the buck along to your manager, i.e., make your boss out to be the mean person who rejected the application. Making tough decisions as a manager is what you get paid the big bucks for.

(The term passing the buck originated from a token, called a buck, which was passed along to the next card dealer.)

Similarly, if your boss asks you to action something, be professional when you pass it along to your staff. Another sport saying is to "Play with a straight bat". Explain the rationale for the decision or request, even if you do not necessarily agree with it.

"When my boss asked me to conduct an audit, I should have handled it more tactfully. I told the staff that my boss had asked me to conduct the audit. This upset the staff, as they had bullying claims against him. My boss was livid with me".

Don't Wait to Be Spoon-Fed

"I worked on a very high profile project. My new subordinate was sitting there saying that our managers needed to tell us exactly what they wanted. So…I told him that we could not wait to be spoon-fed. Yes, I upset him. However, once he understood that I was actually empowering him, we didn't look back".

Managers do not have time to get into the minutia. They are generally far removed from the frontline, day-to-day churn of the business. Therefore, they are not usually best placed to recommend new processes. If they did, the frontline staff would likely readily find fault in the direction and say that the managers should have asked the frontline staff.

The frontline staff are generally the subject matter experts in the contemporary, on-the-ground procedures. Therefore, the frontline staff should make workable recommendations, for endorsement by management (i.e., not wait to be spoon-fed).

Make a Glass

You may be asked to provide coordinated comment on behalf of your work area. I found that, when I called for comment, from my peers, such as planning suggestions, I got little to no response. Instead, if I formulated something and circulated it, I found that others were more likely to comment on it.

Therefore, if I asked what shape I should make a glass, I would get no response. Whereas, if I made a glass and asked what others thought of it, they were more likely to tell me how I could improve it.

This approach seems similar to the humorous advice that if you are ever lost, sit down and start playing the card game, called Patience or Solitaire. Soon, someone is sure to come along and tell you what card move you should be playing.

All Care and No Responsibility

It is really important to nominate specific people to be responsible for performing tasks. If you do not, people will be able to say that they believed someone else was going to do it (all care and no responsibility). This is particularly so if you send an email to a generic email account.

"This principle is similar to the bystander effect, where the presence of others inhibits a person's willingness to help. For example, people standing around watching at an accident scene thinking that others will assist".

Problem Shared = Problem Halved

As the saying goes, a problem shared is a problem halved. Don't just sit on a problem, or pretend it isn't there. Raise the issue as soon as you become aware of it. Even if you just let your boss know that you have identified it, you are working on it and you will give them a briefing, as soon as you have more information. Personally, I always appreciated it when people came to me with a problem and the solution, at the same time. Not just a problem.

When issues arise or things go wrong, a positive outcome could be that it is the impetus for change, i.e., it can assist to create a "sense of urgency", which is step one of Kotter's Eight-Step Change Model. Definitely, do not try to cover the problem up, as this generally makes matters worse. Trying to cover the problem up may make you complicit and liable.

"I created a problem-solving committee, which was attended by council bylaws, the Department of Human Services, police, etc. The meeting was incredibly collaborative. Any attendee could table a community safety related issue. Once issues were tabled, everyone chipped in with actions to resolve the issue".

Do Not Reply (Yet!)

When someone sends you a cranky, misunderstood or similar email, fight the urge to reply immediately. Be the better person. Even if the email sender is behaving badly, if you respond in the same fashion, you are no better than them.

"Do not make a 'Fundamental attribution error'. Do not assume the worse of the email sender and think that their actions reflect their personality, rather than the circumstances. An example would be, if someone toots their car horn and you instantly think that they are arrogant or abusive, when they may be tooting their car horn to say hello or warn you of danger".

Just as people learn differently (e.g., from reading, visually, listening or doing), there may be another explanation for the email. English may be the email sender's second language. The email sender may not have meant how you read the email, or how they wrote it. The email sender may be having a bad day, be ill or be having family trouble. The email sender may already regret sending the email and be sweating, waiting for your response. Alternatively, the email may not have even been sent by that person. Speak to the email sender in person. One option if the email sender is your subordinate is to send a reply email with "Please see me re this email".

Traction on Actions

You are likely to hold several meetings as a manager. You will need to get traction on the action items that you allocate.

"Most of us have attended meetings where there is no update on the action items. For example, the nominated person is on holidays and their representative has no knowledge of the action item".

Some ways that you can get traction on action items are as follows:

- nominate a specific person to complete the action;
- before allocating the action item, confirm that the nominee will be able to complete the task and is available to attend the next meeting;
- advise the nominee to brief any attending representative;
- send the action item list immediately after the meeting; and
- seek updates on the action items days before the next meeting.

Look People in the Eye

If it is a viable option, always choose to speak to people face to face. You will be better able to build relationships, trust and rapport. It is difficult not to bond with someone who is looking directly at you. Furthermore, as the majority of communication is non-verbal being able to see someone's body language is important. When you meet with people, you will be able to better explain tasks and assess comprehension. You can always confirm the meeting outcome in a subsequent email.

Meetings for Meetings' Sake?

It is tempting to cancel meetings when you don't have much for the agenda. However, when you get work people together, even for a social function, they cannot help but talk about work. Nonetheless, I never saw the point in meetings that were talkfests which didn't seem to get anything achieved.

"I made my regular management meetings extremely productive. I formulated a standing agenda, with overarching headings, that covered every area of the business. For example, staff welfare, management update, budget, initiatives, stakeholder engagement/feedback, etc. The standing agenda saved time by not having to type up a new agenda for every meeting. I raised the topics and any attendee could talk on the topic. If no one had anything to contribute, we would move on.

"The meetings gave my staff a voice, a regular arena to raise concerns and share information. When my staff raised issues, I was able to steer the direction. My staff learnt how I thought and what I wanted. I only recorded the action items and important decisions.

"The meetings helped build sound relationships. The managers from the different work areas had to think at my level, covering all of their areas, not just think about their own area and view the other work areas as their opposition".

These management meetings ensured that I wasn't waiting for my manager to send out lists of outstanding tasks. I was proactively, regularly, managing the business, through good governance processes.

Pick Your Battles

Don't sweat the small stuff. Not everything will be, or should be, exactly how you want it. You may lose the battle but win the war.

"When a group of youths were told to leave an address by police, as the youth walked off, they yelled abuse. The police could have taken offense, gone after the youth, and the situation could have escalated. Instead, the police let the youth walk away. When you think about it, the police were achieving their aim. The youth were doing what was asked of them. The youth were only venting and exercising what little power they had".

Is It Really a Social Function?

Social functions may lawfully be deemed to be an extension of the workplace. You, as the manager, and your organisation may be found liable for the conduct that occurs at a function. Consequently, where a social function is being planned by your staff, make sure that you are active in trying to mitigate the risks. For example, remind staff of appropriate behaviour, safe transport, designated drivers, responsible alcohol consumption and even consider having dedicated security staff.

Be Aware of Behaviours

As a manager, you should be aware of workplace behaviours, such as white-anting, leadership styles and procrastination.

a) <u>White-Anting</u>

Some people may be white-anted, i.e., kept out of the loop or information flow. People may go around them to do things, block, ostracise or spread rumours about them. People may treat them like this because they feel that the person:

- is not a team player;
- cannot be trusted;
- would not contribute; or
- would block their initiatives, etc.

b) <u>Leadership Styles</u>

People have default leadership styles. For example, someone could be task-focused or people-focused. Different leadership styles may mean that people want to "get it right", "get it done", "get along" or "get appreciated". If someone is too people-focused, they may not deliver. They may prioritise socialising and relationships and fail to hold people to account for delivery of tasks.

Conversely, if someone is too task-focused, they may not collaborate or consult well. Task-focused people could receive complaints, upset others and demotivate staff. Task-focused people could contribute to creating human resources issues, which require significant time to manage. There is little point in getting a task done and leaving a trail of injured people, who now need to be dealt with. When people respond to a promotion announcement, they usually say that the selectee is a good person. They don't usually say that the selectee has achieved or delivered a lot.

Once you have identified someone's default leadership style, you will be able to better manage and task them. For example, who would you give a memo, that required a response by close of business, to? Who would you choose to get others onboard an idea?

c) Organisational Psychopaths

Some organisations or positions attract power-hungry, organisational psychopaths. They interview well because they are full of self-belief, importance and ideas. However, they lack compassion and empathy. Organisational psychopaths commonly receive complaints that they are a bully. "My boss used to frequently say that sometimes you have to 'burn' people". One trait of an organisational psychopath is to sabotage their victim's avenue of complaint, by pre-emptively undermining their victim's credibility with their own boss.

You can inadvertently attract an organisational psychopath with a poorly worded job advertisement. "Have you ever noticed that police recruitment campaigns can lean more towards helping people than enforcement, control, etc?"

Once organisational psychopaths are in an organisation, they can be extremely difficult to get rid of. One way to remove an organisational psychopath is to appeal to their ego. Play to their desire to make big changes, have a massive impact and drive organisational change. Attract the organisational psychopath to a project position. This can actually remove their line control over many staff. Their substantive position could then be made redundant. For more information on organisational psychopaths and the like, you could read a very interesting book entitled *Working with Monsters*, by John Clarke.

d) Procrastination

Unfortunately, some people seem to find it difficult to make a decision. Some means of deferral or procrastination are to:

- seek additional unrelated information;
- refer the matter to someone else to review (particularly a disinterested party);
- request the establishment of a working party;
- request additional consultation; or
- pass the decision making on to their reliever, when they go on leave.

Managers may procrastinate if they don't understand the issue. Therefore, it may be best to meet with your manager to explain and hand them a report, rather than just send them a report.

I worked on a huge project where the direction kept changing. The project team were continually asked to write additional reports by the executive steering committee, which we weren't members of. I felt like we were running in a rat run, or sitting on an exercise bike, churning out reports. It was as though management were procrastinating and dreaming up what ridiculous reports they could request from us next. Have you ever watched a show called *Idiot Abroad*, where they send someone into wild places? That is what it felt like.

Walk the Floor

As I am task-focused, a very wise manager once told me to "put people at the top of your to-do list". Consequently, once I finished writing my "to-do" list, at the start of each day, I walked around and talked to staff. As a bonus, once I returned to my desk, after walking the floor, I could write off several of my tasks because I had already completed them by speaking to people.

Walking the floor helped address a common complaint about managers, being their lack of visibility and approachability. Speaking with staff gave me insight into the current issues that they were facing. I could use these examples to steer the management direction. I could sort out emerging issues in a timely way. I could put out spot fires, rather than having to fight a blaze when the issue was eventually escalated to management.

Walking the floor allowed me to share corporate news and strategic direction. Even if other nearby staff were not engaged in the conversation, they were watching and listening (perhaps more intently than if you gathered them in for a presentation). "When I was leaving a workplace, someone told me that they didn't really know me, but they often overheard me speaking nicely to staff".

I believe that spending time with staff makes them feel valued, consulted, connected and heard. If you don't make the effort to speak to people, they can make assumptions that you are aloof, arrogant, etc.

Forgiveness or Permission?
(Opt Out or Opt In)

There is a saying that sometimes it is better to ask for forgiveness than permission. I found that, sometimes, it is easier to just implement a change, rather than seek permission to implement it.

"I sought permission to introduce a form that I had drafted. My boss sat on the file and then handed it to her replacement when she went on holiday. Her replacement zealously attached a wordy, covering memo, directing me to conduct additional research, consult further, etc., etc. (See the 'Be aware of behaviours' principle which covers Procrastination). I completed his requests but did not resubmit the file for endorsement (opt in). Instead, I introduced the form 'as a trial'. If my manager had wanted to, she could have put the brakes on the trial (opt out). In that case, I would have had to beg her for forgiveness".

Ready, Fire! Aim?

My wise rotary mentor introduced me to the saying, "Ready, Fire, Aim". (I know, it looks like I have incorrectly written it, but I haven't.) My mentor's explanation was that you can spend lots of time planning to do something (Ready), but, at some stage, you have to just do it (Fire).

Even with substantial planning, things can go awry. You need to monitor the change and be prepared to make adjustments along the way (Aim). This is similar to "action research", where action and research are undertaken simultaneously. My point is not to get stuck in the planning phase. Start. There is a sport's saying that "you miss 100% of the shots you don't take". Once you start shooting for the hoop, you can adjust how you are shooting, depending on where the shots are going.

The Purse Strings

Do your best to understand and navigate the corporate finances, even if you think it is boring, or that you don't have a head for it. Learn how to make purchases. I learnt that you can have a delegation (an authorisation to spend a certain amount), but that doesn't mean that the money is available. Even if the funds are there, it doesn't mean that the funds haven't already been committed. Furthermore, you can be given funds for a specific project, but that doesn't mean that that is what the money will be spent on.

"I was on a major project, which was fully funded, but my boss made it almost impossible for us to spend any of the allocated funds. He kept making us justify the expenditure. It was as though the money went into Grandma's purse, to buy us treats, but then Grandma had discretion as to whether we had been good and if that was what the money would be spent on. I think other areas of the organisation stuck their hands into the purse and there were almost no funds left for the given purpose".

The thinking was, as long as we delivered what the money was given to us for, it didn't matter that the money was used for another purpose. Whilst this process was somewhat bewildering to me, I guess that it would be difficult to separate and account for monies or tie the purse strings of a giant organisation.

At the end of the financial year, all budget lines can be rolled into one. Therefore, areas that had surplus money lost it to cover areas that had overspent. Even if money was allocated for a specific project, you had to fight to have it carried over into the next financial year.

"One area that I know of paid a large sum of money, in advance, to a well-known external software provider, at the end of the financial year, rather than lose the project funds. Perhaps unsurprisingly, once the money was paid, the external provider seemed to lose interest in fixing the program's bugs (issues)".

On a separate occasion, "I was asked to examine why we had overspent on a contract. My investigation revealed that there was never enough money being put into the budget line to cover the known cost of the signed contract!"

Use the Red Tape

Generally, I do not like overcomplicating processes. However, there appears to be a place for it. There are times when introducing additional hurdles (red tape) may be beneficial.

"When the budget was extremely tight, a process was introduced so expenditures, over a very low amount, had to be referred to a committee for approval. The process caused substantial delay and therefore, very effectively reduced expenditure".

"Similarly, in times of fiscal constraint, a committee was established to approve the advertisement of vacancies. A business case had to be submitted to the committee to justify advertising a vacancy. The committee only sat once a month. This process delayed the hiring of staff and therefore, led to the organisation saving a significant amount of money. (I can only assume that other staff worked harder to get the work done and attended to any urgent work.)"

Fix It Now and in the Future

"When I transferred to a new position, I sat next to another manager. I was there to help him. However, he was too busy to even talk to me. I watched him work frantically. It was as though he was spinning around wildly batting away queries. However, as he had no structure, the balls kept coming at him. The manager was dealing with issues, but not addressing them strategically, to reduce his future workload. He did not take the time to think about how he could avoid the same issues from reoccurring".

Things will go wrong, but once they do, you should take steps to ensure that something similar does not occur again. Doing so should protect you, and your organisation, from tortuous (and torturous) litigation. Otherwise, if you fail to take steps to mitigate foreseeable risks, you may be found to be negligent.

"For example, if someone gets injured, you do nothing, and someone else gets injured in the same way, you may be liable. A good workplace safety framework to consider, for possible resolution options, is the workplace hazard 'Hierarchy of control'. It contains strategies to reduce the risk (e.g., removing, replacing or isolating the hazard, changing the way people work, or protecting the worker with personal protection equipment)".

Email Bail (Liberation)

"I routinely checked my emails, at home, in my own time, which was not healthy. I felt like I was hooked up to an intravenous drip with my phone constantly feeding me emails".

As a manager, you will need to implement strategies to manage your emails. Some managers put an "out of office" reply on when they went on leave, advising people that, because they were on leave, their email would be automatically deleted. Other managers would manually delete all the emails that were sent to them whilst they were on leave. Personally, to manage my own emails, I decided that I would not action them if I was only cc'd into them.

To assist you to manage your emails, at the very least, you should ensure that your staff briefly summarise the email chain and state why they sent the email to you. Your staff should not make you read the whole email chain and then have to guess why they sent the email to you.

Avoid "Scope Creep"

When you try to implement a change, others may want to increase the scope of your work. If you allow the scope to extend too far, the change will become unwieldy and impossible to achieve. It is best to set the parameters at the start of the project and have them endorsed by management. That way, you can refer to the approved scope to determine if an additional request falls within it.

Induction Instruction

It is easy, when you are busy, not to prioritise properly inducting new employees. However, inductions are vitally important to set the workplace culture and expectations. You should have a current induction document which you give to your new staff and go through with them. How can you hold someone accountable for something that they were never told?

Vile Files

You need to establish rules to manage files. I always wanted to be spoken to before being given a new initiative file. I did not want my staff spending time unnecessarily creating a file, which I knew wasn't going to be supported. Where I could, I actioned verbal requests immediately, without the need for a file to be created.

If a file had to be submitted to me, for forwarding on, I did not want to have to do any research on the file, or type a covering memo. I wanted the file to have a cover sheet attached, that:

- briefly summarised the purpose of the file;
- stated where the file needed to be sent;
- specified a person, from the area that the file was going to, who had been consulted and who was expecting the file;
- referenced the relevant policy; and
- only needed my endorsement and signature.

File Piles

Think about your file allocation. Do you always give files to your dependable, hard workers and let others get away with not doing files? If so, you could burn out your hard workers and not upskill others.

"When I started in a new role, I was astounded to see incomplete, easy, files, that were a couple of years old. I started churning through the work and completing files. As soon as I finished files, I was given more files. Then, I realised what was going on. Others were sitting on their files so they were not given more files. The file allocation system was actually a deterrent to staff completing files.

"I know of another process where staff took matters as they came along a virtual conveyor belt. However, difficult files were obvious. Consequently, everyone waited for someone else to take the difficult file. Once they did, the others immediately took the following easy files".

Difficult Conversations

Some conversations are difficult, but you need to have them. Be honest but tactful. You have to balance staff welfare and performance management. It is best to start performance discussions by asking questions (how the staff are, how they think they are travelling, is there anything that is affecting their current performance, etc.) That gives your staff an opportunity to advise you if something is adversely affecting their performance. Otherwise, you would feel terrible if you launched into how poorly they were working, and then they divulged that they have cancer, had just separated, etc. Also, be mindful of the setting for the conversation. You should praise in public and only criticise in private.

Individual Meetings

It is important to have individual meetings with your direct reports. I had one-on-one meetings with my subordinates, which included the following:

1. <u>them</u> – how they were travelling, how I could assist their career development, etc.;
2. <u>their staff</u> – any issues that their staff were experiencing;
3. <u>initiatives</u> – new activities to continue to grow the business; and
4. <u>me</u> – any feedback that they may have in relation to how I could improve.

Be There

In times of tragedy, be with your staff. Be visible. For example, attend funerals when your staff lose family members. Be there to support your staff, even if there is absolutely nothing that you can do to assist. There are many examples of leaders attending disaster scenes and pictures of leaders standing publicly with their people in times of crisis.

There are also examples of leaders being criticised for being absent. "During the Black Saturday bushfires in Victoria, the then chief commissioner was criticised for being absent from her post. Even though, there may have been very little that she could have done to prevent those tragic deaths".

"The following headline, published in the Australian Daily Mail, appears to be another example of the need to 'Be there', even when there is little that might have been able to be done. It relates to an allegation that the premier was absent during a pandemic. 'Dan Andrews is slammed for refusing to cancel his holiday plans as a third Covid outbreak threatens Victoria'".

You should never underestimate the impact that your support and kindness can have on someone. There is a lovely tale about a person who walks along a beach filled with washed-up starfish. When the person starts throwing starfish back into the ocean, their companion says that they can't make a difference because there are too many stranded starfish. The person replied that they are making a difference to each starfish that they throw back in.

How Do You Eat an Elephant?

There is a saying "How do you eat an elephant?" The answer is "One bite at a time". This applies in business. Large projects can seem overwhelming. You need to break large tasks into smaller, manageable tasks and chip away at achieving them. Some of the smaller, easier tasks may be described as "quick wins" or "low hanging fruit". These tasks can be completed relatively easily. Completion of "quick wins" creates a sense of accomplishment, which inspires staff to continue their efforts. Before you know it, you will have made significant headway on the large task.

"When I commenced a new role, I was given the Occupational Health and Safety (OHS) portfolio. It had been many months since an OHS meeting had been held, in contravention of the legislation, so I set to work. We soon had safety briefings, regular OHS meetings, electronic safety messaging, safety debriefs, safety investigations, etc. It wasn't long before our work unit received the chief executive officer's highly competitive, safety award".

As stated, small actions can roll up into the achievement of bigger tasks. Have you heard people say that they do not have good key selection criteria examples for their job applications? Well, they probably would if they put them under umbrella titles. For example, if they specified what they have cumulatively achieved to develop staff, to save costs, to create efficiencies or to improve stakeholder engagement or customer service.

Create the Focus

It is the role of executive managers to set the corporate direction. However, the executive managers do not have to have all of the answers regarding exactly how the objectives will be met. It is incredible what staff can achieve once they know what the objective or focus is. Consequently, you need to make sure that your staff know what you stand for and what you want to achieve. To use another sport analogy, most staff are eager, ready and willing to kick the ball, once they know where the goalposts are.

"For example, one Victoria Police Chief Commissioner publicly stated that she wanted to reduce vehicle thefts by 10 percent, but she did not specify exactly how that was to occur. The statement created the focus. It empowered staff to suggest innovative ways to reduce vehicle thefts. It also lead to competition among staff to achieve the objective in the best and fastest way possible".

Cause and Effect

There is much support for the contention that, when you act in response to an issue or make a change, you can inadvertently create additional issues, or possibly worse complications. (For example, the Ripple Effect, the Butterfly Effect, Newton's Third Law of Action and Reaction, and The Law of Unintended Consequences.)

"For example, if you conduct a police operation to target crime, you may cause temporal or geographical displacement, i.e., you may see an increase in crime at another time of the day, or at another location".

If you introduce onerous processes or objectives, it may cause your staff to cut corners and take the path of least resistance. "Have you ever noticed a meandering path which has a well-worn shortcut?" This proposition appears consistent with the Age headline on 4 September 2019 "Police cut breath test target after 'falsies' scandal".

There's More Than One Way to Skin a Cat

I am definitely not talking about animal cruelty. I am saying that there are generally several ways to do things. You should put time and effort into considering the smartest way to achieve your desired outcome. You should always tell the truth, but there is a difference between being brutally honest and being tactful. "As a child, I didn't understand the distinction". With forethought, you can balance telling the truth, trying not to hurt people, not inflaming situations and achieving your aim.

I always like to work smarter, not harder. Here is a story about someone smartly achieving their objective that my eldest son relayed to me…A mother told her young child to brush their teeth. The child refused. So, the mother said, "Okay, well, I am going to brush my teeth first then". Immediately, the child raced to brush their teeth and make sure that their mum did not win the teeth brushing competition.

Close the Window First

The "Close the window first" principle relates to responding to an issue. There is little point in cleaning up water that has come inside from an open window, if it is still raining outside, the window is still open and there is still water coming in.

When an issue is identified, some people get bogged down with determining how they should respond to the damage caused by the issue before they do anything to address the issue itself. I do not see much point in assessing or cleaning up damage while damage is still occurring. You should close the window first.

"For example, if staff are not following a process, you should advise the staff to cease their current practice immediately". I know that this may seem difficult. As soon as you send out such an instruction, the issue may become public knowledge. You may need to face the media and answer questions about the scale of the issue and what you are going to do about it.

If you are asked for media comment, it may be reasonable to say that you have just identified the issue, you are going to assess the impact, determine the most appropriate response and you will keep them apprised. If you have delayed responding to the issue, you are likely to be asked when you first became aware of the issue and the reason for the delay. Imagine if you delayed a safety-related product recall? However, you may not want to comment if the matter is subject to an active or ongoing investigation. Also, you may not want to admit liability if it might increase the likelihood of a successful lawsuit against you, or your organisation.

The K.I.S. Principle

I could not write this book without including the principle of "Keeping It Simple". The K.I.S. principle relates to not overcomplicating things. For example, some of the most effective brand slogans are extremely basic.

Once an organisation becomes large, it is often difficult for management to convey key messages to the frontline workers. Nowadays, there is so much information that it is easy for important information to get swamped and lost in the sea of information. People can get overwhelmed and overlook important messages.

Unfortunately, some people seem to think that they have to write swaths of text to justify their worth. However, if you write a wordy policy, for example, what you are telling people to do may not even be that obvious. Consequently, when you are writing, ask yourself "What am I trying to achieve?"; "What is the key message?" and "Who needs to hear it?" If you keep your messaging simple, your message is likely to be more readily understood and complied with.

Centralise/Decentralise

If you stay in an organisation long enough, you will see patterns occurring and history repeating. This may occur with centralising funds or staff and then decentralising funds or staff again (Centralise/decentralise).

History repeating:

- happens with fashion too. Just after I threw out my motley brown leather jacket, that had hung in my wardrobe for many years, they came back into fashion;
- means that, as part of good risk management, organisations should:
    - undertake environmental scanning, to see what issues are arising in other companies, and check if they have them too; and
    - randomly check to see if any significant issues that have arisen in the past have resurfaced.

"An example of issues repeating may be Victoria Police receiving significant media attention over repeated issues with delegations".

What's Your Legacy?

What have you achieved in your organisation? How have you made a difference? If others had to give your work eulogy, what would they say about what you have done? Think about this when you start a new job and whilst you go about your day-to-day work. These achievements are what you would highlight in job applications and panels.

The Egg in the Fry Pan

Visualise a simple aerial drawing of a cracked egg, frying in a fry pan. This can be related to you and your influence. The egg yolk represents what you can directly control. The egg white represents what you can influence. The fry pan represents what is outside your control. You have to know your limits. Do what you can, but do not be hard on yourself for being unable to do everything.

You Catch More Flies
with Honey

The proverb "You get more flies with honey, than with vinegar" means that you are more likely to get what you want by being nice and sweet, rather than being sour and bitter. This applies in business relationships too. You should be nice. As a manager, you could always escalate if you needed to. If you come on too strong in the first instance, it is difficult to deescalate. You may have already lost your audience. Just because you have power, doesn't mean that you have to use it. In fact, it may show more strength to exercise restraint and not use your power. This contention seems consistent with the phrase, "If you want to test a person's character, give them power".

Win-Win

This relates to a negotiation where each party gets something out of the resolution that they want (win-win). Win-win is what you should try to achieve. It is of great assistance in deliberations if you can find common objectives. You should also consider relevant, independent information sources. You may start with what you think is a good idea, but this can often be built on to become a better idea, with additional consultation. The keys to achieving win-win outcomes are compromise and cooperation.

Gender Equity

As a manager, you should know that if someone starts from a disadvantaged position, treating everyone the same doesn't address the disadvantage gap. Disadvantaged people need to be treated differently to address the disadvantage gap.

When people are absent from the workplace for a significant period (e.g., on maternity leave) they are likely to be disadvantaged (e.g., by losing currency with their networks, skills, processes, experience and self-confidence). As a biological fact, this workplace absence is more likely to occur with women due to pregnancy and breastfeeding.

Women may also be disadvantaged in the workplace in other ways. Have you ever watched reality television shows where they vote people out? If so, have you noticed that the women get voted out first? When a child is sick which parent will the school default to calling first?

Anyway, ultimately, my point is, for a variety of reasons, there seems to be merit in assisting women in the workplace. "For example, I liked to give pregnant women professional development opportunities to try and compensate for their immanent, extended absence from the workplace".

The Old and the New

The old and the new relates to the challenge of changing over to new systems and processes. When you are trying to work on a new system and keep an old system running and up-to-date, it can be very difficult and time consuming. An example of this would be if you had hard copy files and were moving to using electronic files. Additional work is usually required from staff during the changeover period. You may want to consider paying overtime, or hiring temporary staff, during the changeover period. This should minimise disruption and get the change introduced as quickly as possible.

The Full Cup

There is a story about a teacher who filled a glass cup with rocks and asked the students if the cup was full. When the students said that the cup was full, the teacher added pebbles and asked the students again if the cup was full. When the students said that the cup was full, the teacher added sand and again asked the students if the cup was full. When the students said that the cup was full, the teacher poured his coffee into the cup. The teacher said the lesson was, no matter how full your life seems, there is always room for a cup of coffee, i.e., do not get so bogged down in your work that you do not take your breaks. Take some time to enjoy a cup of coffee with others. (Besides, it's a great networking opportunity!)

From Generosity to Expectation

There will be times when you are asked to provide staff to another work area. For example, to assist with a certain task, or as a professional development opportunity. There will be an expectation that you will be a "good corporate citizen" and release your staff. However, think carefully before releasing your staff. Your supply of staff can quickly turn from being an act of generosity to an expectation that your work area continues to provide the staff.

"After my staff member's secondment period ended, it was argued that they needed to stay, because they had unfinished work, they had developed expertise in the role, and continuity in the role was required. When I refused to let them stay, the matter was escalated to my boss, who dictated that my staff must stay".

"When I arrived as a manager of a work area, there were long-standing, mandatory secondments of my staff elsewhere. Despite me trying very hard, I was unable to get my manager to cease the mandatory secondments. I would have been better off if the staff had been transferred to the other work area, permanently, i.e., I was responsible for the seconded staff's administration and supplying a backfill when they took leave".

"Annoyingly, these secondments meant that the formula, for determining who would get more staff, was unfairly applied. The formula was applied as if I had the staff and as if the other work area didn't have the staff. Therefore, the other work area received additional permanent staff, I didn't, and the secondments continued!"

Even if it is agreed that other work areas will share the staffing obligation, when it is their turn, they will have excuses why they cannot supply their staff. Therefore, try not to be the first one to supply staff. If you do supply staff, specify tight parameters for the secondment, within a written Memorandum of Understanding.

If you commence in a new role and ascertain that you are supplying staff to another work area, work with your manager and give notice, as soon as you can, that you need your staff back. Even if you have to extend the timeframe, it will be better than leaving your staff there on an ongoing basis. The longer that you lend your staff out, the more difficult it is to say that you cannot do without them (because you are continuing to prove that you can do without them, with every day that passes!).

Resources Should Follow the Work

If a new task is given to your work unit, the proportionate resources (staff) should be given to your work unit too. (The exception would be if a workload analysis had been undertaken and the task was being transferred for a more equitable workload distribution.)

Staff should be provided with the task, even where the task is only "temporarily" transferred to your work unit, i.e., it is highly possible that you will end up having to do the task on an ongoing basis (See the principle "From generosity to expectation"). It is harder to argue that you have insufficient staff to undertake the task when your staff have already been doing the task.

Where resources are taken from your establishment, to create another work unit, with a particular charter, be watchful that the work does not creep back to your work unit and the resources remain at the new work unit. (It pays to know the background of work unit establishment and to keep good records.)

Put a Bow on It

This principle relates to wrapping up files nicely. Files should be packaged up in a way that anyone who picks the file up next can readily understand the background, status and next steps. This protects your reputation. Many files go awry upon a change of hands. Previous file holders can be blamed for not passing on vital information. Therefore, a summary should be included on the file to reflect the status of the file upon a change of hands (Put a bow on it).

"I worked on a large annual legal publication contract. I assumed that I would be undertaking the task again the next year. Consequently, I did not put a summary on the file or tidy it up. However, when the contract renewal approached, I was in a different role and on leave. The file was taken from my office and the task was given to someone else. The file was not organised, neat and tidy. The file condition would have reflected poorly on me. The file condition did not reflect the amount of effort and care that I had taken with the task, or that I usually take with my work. As I got wiser as a manager, whenever I went on leave, I typed up an email handover for my reliever and copied my boss into the email".

Mirror, Mirror

Most of us have heard the tale of "Snow White", which has the magic mirror that gives feedback. The "mirror, mirror" principle relates to you and your presence, personal impact. There is usually a difference in how you see yourself and how others see you. As part of good leadership, you should try to understand and improve how others see you. Part of the rationale for this is that you need to have the interpersonal skills to persuade your management team for the benefit of your staff. So, could you be seen as talking over people, predominately talking about yourself, as being inflexible, being too quiet, or talking too much, etc.?

Be a Media Star

You need to know how to manage the media. I used to think that I was at the mercy of the media, unsure of what question they might ask me. I now know that the interviewee can actually be in control of the interview. You should prepare and memorise key talking points in advance. When you are asked a question, you should use a bridging phrase and answer the question with your talking points. Politicians are particularly skilled at this. They may use bridging phrases like, "That is not what I am here to talk about, what I want to talk about is…or what I can say is…"

When you prepare your key talking points, work out the best way to respond to an issue. "For example, if a police chief commissioner was caught speeding, they could highlight that no one is above the law and that it demonstrates that even the most careful of drivers can make a mistake. (If you readily admit fault, fall on your sword, it generally gives interviewers less ammunition, takes the wind out of their sails.)"

Don't Create a Rod for Your Own Back

Try not to create additional, unnecessary work for yourself in the future (create a rod for your own back). You should draft documents to require as little future amendment as possible when there are changes in the organisation, such as staff turnover. One way of doing this is to specify positions in an instruction, rather than to name specific people. For example, applications should be submitted to the Manager, Operations (not Joe Johns).

Where something is likely to change regularly, use a link to the up-to-date online document. I prefer this rather than emailing a document around every time it is amended. I also like version dates on documents, so everyone readily knows if they are referring to the same version of a document.

I don't recommend specifying that a policy will be reviewed in a certain timeframe. We all get busy and may not be able to prioritise reviewing a policy that there may be no issue with. I prefer to state that the policy will stand, unless revoked or updated and specify a process for advising if the policy requires updating.

No Marching Band

You could throw yourself into work and work long hours to the detriment of family time. If you do, you may think that: the organisation will fall down when you leave; the business will not go on without you; and when you leave, there will be an enormous send-off (with a marching band!). Well, there won't be. This is not about being negative. This is about being practical. Do not be a work martyr. The organisation will go on. Work will continue. There will be plenty of people eager to come into the organisation. Whether you have a function, or not, will depend on whether you have a friend who is thoughtful and organised enough to arrange it. Balance your life. Be a well-rounded person. You set an example for your staff. Have outside interests. When you retire, you should have something else to occupy you. I do not think many people on their deathbed would say that they wished they had worked more. Enjoy your life, family and friends (Take the time to smell the roses!).

In Conclusion

In summary, a good manager needs to have a variety of skills. This book has provided practical suggestions to assist managers to:

- maintain corporate awareness;
- consult wisely;
- support their staff;
- monitor work completion;
- treat everyone with respect;
- act with due consideration;
- show initiative;
- establish efficient structures and processes;
- deliver on tasks;
- identify and manage risks;
- market their achievements; and
- manage their own time and wellbeing.

Generous comment by Kiara Hutchinson, "Thanks for the great read!"

Glowing review by Daniel James Tate, "It wasn't terrible".

Keen observation by Max Vandersteen, "I like the red tape, it is smart".